Little Book of

EMBROIDERED
GARDEN FLOWERS

Diana Lampe

SALLY MILNER PUBLISHING
(MILNER CRAFT SERIES)

First published in 1999 by

Sally Milner Publishing Pty Ltd

P. O. Box 2104

Bowral NSW 2576

Australia

Reprinted 1999

© Diana Lampe, 1999

Design by Anna Warren, Warren Ventures, Sydney

Photography by John Tucker, Canberra

Printed and bound in China

National Library of Australia

Cataloguing-in-Publication data

Lampe, Diana.

Little book of embroidered garden flowers.

Includes index.

ISBN 1 86351 226 8

1. Embroidery - Patterns. 2. Decoration and ornament -
Plant forms. I. Title. (Series : Milner craft series).

746.44

$\mathcal{L}$ist of $\mathcal{F}$lowers

HELPFUL HINTS FOR FLOWER DESIGNS

• Diagrams and embroidered samples are reproduced actual size.

• Use a 2B pencil to transfer flower designs. Draw freehand or trace from diagrams.

• Left-handed embroiderers. You shouldn't have any trouble with embroidery because you are left-handed. Just reverse the instructions and look at a mirror image of the stitch diagrams. For reference *More Embroidered Garden Flowers* features a left-handed stitch glossary.

Introduction

This little book contains a collection of favourite embroidered flower designs. I have used basic embroidery stitches to work the flowers and if this is your first venture into the world of embroidery you should have no difficulty following the instructions. Embroidery looks very complicated when it is finished, but really it isn't if you take it one step at a time.

I am constantly making little changes and refinements to my embroidered flowers. This may happen when a particular flower is in bloom in my garden, during a class, or when I am working the flowers into a new design. Putting this book together has given me the opportunity to rewrite the instructions and include some new colours and ideas and I have really enjoyed this task.

I find settling down with some embroidery is a most satisfying way to spend time and I hope you will find this too and enjoy stitching these flowers. Please read through the section entitled *Basic Requirements* before you start.

DIANA LAMPE, 1999

$\mathcal{B}$asic $\mathcal{R}$equirements

FABRIC

I like to use a good quality embroidery linen for my embroidery. It is firm to work with and will last longer than other fabrics. Other suitable fabrics to use are silk, damask or unbleached calico. If you choose silk, use a light cotton backing to add body. Wash the fabric before you use it, in case it shrinks.

NEEDLES

Choose a good quality needle that takes the thread easily. The needle has to make a hole in the fabric for the thread to pass through. If it is too small you will find it difficult to thread and hard to pull through the fabric. A needle that is too big will result in coarse stitching whereas a smaller needle will help keep your work fine.

Embroidery crewel needles are used for most embroidery stitches, as the sharp point and large eye make them easy to work with. However, a straw or millinery needle should always be used for working bullion stitch. The long shaft and small eye will pass through the wraps easily resulting in an even bullion stitch. To work the flowers in this book use: No. 7 crewel or straw needle for 3 or 4 strands of thread; No. 8 or 9 crewel or straw needle for 2 strands of thread; No. 9 or 10 crewel or straw needle for 1 strand of thread.

MARKING PENCIL

A soft lead pencil (2B) should be used rather than any other kind of marker. Some markers leave a chemical residue in the fabric, which could reappear or may rot the fabric in the future. Be sure your pencil is sharp and keep pencil marks light so they can be removed easily when you wash the finished embroidery. If you need to change the pencil marks, use an Artgum or fabric eraser.

THREADS

DMC stranded cotton (embroidery floss) has been used for the designs in this book. It is a mercerised six-stranded cotton thread and can be separated into the required number of strands.

Do not cut thread too long. A good length to use is 40 to 45 cm (16" to 18").

It is important to strip the thread before embroidering, to aerate the strands and ensure smooth coverage when the stitches are worked. This means separating all the individual strands of your cut thread, and then putting back together the number of individual strands you require. To do this, hold the thread at the top and pull the individual strands upward to avoid tangling.

All spun threads should be worked with the grain. The thread will twist and unravel if worked against the grain. Run your fingers down the thread to feel the grain; smooth is with the grain, rough is against it.

Always thread the needle with the end you pull from the DMC skein, which is called the 'blooming end'. If your thread has been sitting awhile the 'blooming end' will have started to unravel.

SCISSORS

A small pair of good quality embroidery scissors with sharp, pointed blades for snipping your threads.

HOOPS

For good tension use a small embroidery hoop [10 cm (4")] for french knots, french knot stalks, colonial knots, couching, and all stitches of the satin stitch family. Wooden hoops should be wrapped with white cotton tape to avoid damaging your work. Do not leave your work in a hoop as it may damage or mark the fabric.

DMC STRANDED COTTONS USED IN THIS BOOK

blanc neige
ecru
208 lavender, very dark
209 lavender, dark
210 lavender, medium
211 lavender, light
315 antique mauve, very dark
316 antique mauve, medium
327 violet, very dark
333 blue violet, dark
340 blue violet, medium
341 blue violet, light
372 mustard, light
444 lemon, dark
452 shell grey, medium
469 avocado green
471 avocado green, very light
503 blue green, medium
522 fern green
550 violet, very dark
552 violet, medium

602 cranberry, medium
603 cranberry
604 cranberry, light
611 drab brown, dark
612 drab brown, medium
640 beige grey, very dark
718 plum
726 topaz, light
727 topaz, very light
743 yellow, medium
745 yellow, light pale
746 off-white
791 cornflower blue, very dark
800 delft, pale
809 delft
840 beige brown, medium
945 sportsman flesh, medium
972 canary, deep
973 canary, bright
3013 khaki green, light

3042 antique violet, light
3045 yellow beige, dark
3051 green grey, dark
3078 golden yellow, very light
3345 hunter green, dark
3346 hunter green
3347 yellow green, medium
3348 yellow green, light
3354 dusty rose, light
3363 pine green, medium
3371 black brown
3607 plum, light
3608 plum, very light
3609 plum, ultra light
3740 antique violet, dark
3746 blue violet, dark
3772 nutmeg, light
3803 rose mauve

$\mathcal{C}$ROCUS

THREADS
973 canary — bright
3346 hunter green

Flowers
2 strands 973. Work small crocus flowers with 3 lazy daisy stitches, slightly overlapping and pointing upwards.

Stems and Leaves
2 strands 3346. Add stems to flowers, and leaves around stems, using straight stitch.

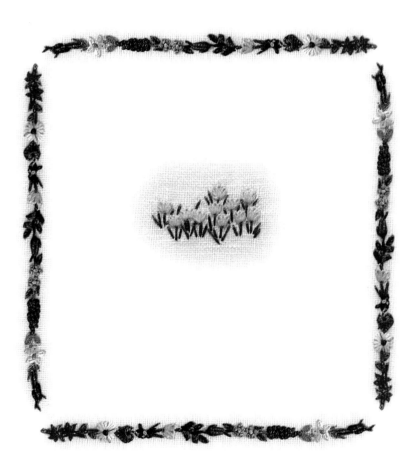

$\mathcal{D}$AFFODIL

THREADS
372 mustard — light
972 canary — deep

973 canary — bright
3363 pine green — medium

Flowers
trumpet — 2 strands 972, buttonhole stitch. Draw a triangle for trumpet of daffodil. Work trumpet with 3 buttonhole stitches, start on left-hand side of lower edge.
petals — 2 strands 973, lazy daisy stitch. Add 2 or 3 lazy daisy stitch petals above trumpet.
front view — Work a tiny buttonhole circle for trumpet. Add 6 evenly spaced petals around trumpet with very short, open lazy daisy stitches (i.e. fly stitch). Fill each petal with a small straight stitch.

Stems and Leaves
2 strands 3363, stem stitch.

Bract
2 strands 372. Add a lazy daisy stitch for bract behind flower at top of stem.

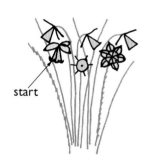

Other colour combinations: 743 and 745; 945 and 746.

$\mathcal{D}$APHNE

THREADS
ecru
315 antique mauve — *very dark*

316 antique mauve — *medium*
840 beige brown — *medium*
3345 hunter green — *dark*

Trunk and Branches
branches — 2 strands 840. Work with long bullion stitch and couch into position. Fit wraps on needle to length of branch.

Buds and Flowers
buds — 2 strands 315.
flowers — 1 strand each ecru and 316 blended. Mark positions for flowers with small circles. Work buds in centre with 2 or 3 french knots in deeper pink and surround with several french knot flowers.

Leaves
2 strands 3345. Add several lazy daisy stitch leaves in varying lengths. Some leaves should overlap branches. Stitch with firm tension and extend little stitch at the end. Add extra leaves to branches throughout the bush where necessary.

$\mathcal{E}$NGLISH PRIMROSE

THREADS

471 avocado green — very light
612 drab brown — medium
745 yellow — light pale

Flowers
petals — 2 strands 745. Mark a spot for centres of flowers. Work the 5-petalled flowers from the centre with small lazy daisy stitches. Work some flowers with only 4 petals to depict a side view.
centre — 2 strands 612, french knot.

Stems
2 strands 471, couching.

Leaves
2 strands 471. Make lazy daisy stitch
leaves a little longer than usual.

$\mathcal{F}$ELICIA OR BLUE MARGUERITE

THREADS
444 lemon — dark
3346 hunter green

3746 blue violet — dark
3772 nutmeg — light

Flowers
petals — 2 strands 3746. Mark small circles with a dot in the centre for daisies. Work petals with straight stitch from outside edge of flower, down into centre. Leave a small space for centre. Work 1 stitch for each quarter and fill in between these with 2 more petals, making 12 petals. Some petals will be stitched into same hole.
centre — 2 strands 444, french knot.

Stems
2 strands 3772, straight stitch.

Leaves
2 strands 3346, lazy daisy stitch.

ℱORGET-ME-NOT

There are three different colours given for the forget-me-not flowers.

THREADS
800 delft — pale
or
809 delft
or

3354 dusty rose — light
also
469 avocado green
726 topaz — light

Flowers
Each flower has a french knot centre with 5 french knot petals.
centre — 2 strands 726. Work french knot centres for flowers first, leaving enough space between them for petals.
petals — 2 strands 800, 809 or 3354.
Surround each centre closely with 5
french knot petals. Petals should touch
the centre.

Leaves
2 strands 469, lazy daisy stitch.

*G*AZANIA OR TREASURE FLOWER

THREADS
522 *fern green*
972 *canary — deep*

973 *canary — bright*
3371 *black brown*

Flower
petals — 2 strands 973. Lightly mark flowers with a tiny circle surrounded by a bigger circle. Work petals from inner circle leaving a small space for the centre. Work a small lazy daisy stitch petal for each quarter and fill in between these with 2 more petals, making 12 petals.
centre — 1 strand 3371 and 3 strands 972. Stitch french knots around inside circle with 3371 then add the centre french knot in 972.
side-view flower — If desired work a side-view flower with 4 or 5 petals and attach it to stem with a tiny fly stitch calyx in 522.

Stems
2 strands 522, straight stitch.

Leaves
2 strands 522, chain stalks. Work leaves back towards stems, in the opposite direction to a lazy daisy stitch.

Note: A chain stalk is a lazy daisy stitch with an extended anchoring stitch.

$\mathscr{G}$RAPE HYACINTH

THREADS
333 blue violet — dark
3347 yellow green — medium

Stems

2 strands 3347, couching. Do not place
these too close to each other as flowers may
merge. Add some leaves if you wish with
backstitch.

Flowers

2 strands 333. Work french knots over and
around stems in a conical shape, tapering to
1 french knot at top.

HEARTSEASE OR JOHNNY JUMP-UP

THREADS
211 lavender — light
444 lemon — dark

469 avocado green
550 violet — very dark
727 topaz — very light

Flowers

These flowers are very tiny, so stitches need to be kept as small as possible. Work 1 or 2 flowers at a time to make it easier to position them. Some flowers may overlap another. Be sure to keep threads not in use on top of your work.

start

lower petals — 2 strands 444. Draw small triangles for lower petals. Work each lower petal with 3 tiny buttonhole stitches. Start stitching at left-hand side of lower edge and work each stitch into same hole in the centre.

top petals and spot — 2 strands 550. From slightly above central point, work two top petals pointing upwards in lazy daisy stitch. Add spot with a french knot to bottom edge of lower petal.

side petals — 1 strand each 727 and 211 blended, lazy daisy stitch. Work side petals at a slightly upward angle. They will overlap the upper petals a little.

Leaves

2 strands 469, lazy daisy stitch.

$\mathcal{H}$YDRANGEA

THREADS

209 lavender — *dark*
211 lavender — *light*
340 blue violet — *medium*
341 blue violet — *light*

471 avocado green — *very light*
3045 yellow beige — *dark*
3346 hunter green
3746 blue violet — *dark*
3348 yellow green — *light*

Branches and Stems

branches — 2 strands 3045, stem stitch.

stems — 2 strands 471, stem stitch. (See colour plate opposite.)

Flowers (see cover)

middle section of flower — 4 strands thread in blends of 209, 211, 340, 341 and 3746, colonial knots.

outer section of flower — 3 strands thread in blends of 209, 211, 340, 341 and 3746, colonial knots.

Draw circular or elliptical flower shapes amongst the branches. Blend threads to vary colour and shade of flowers. (Flowers can be quite blue or more mauve, lighter or darker.) Work middle section of flower first with 4 strands of blended threads in colonial knots. Fill rest with colonial knots in 3 strands. Stitch colonial knots in formation, i.e. in rows across or around flower.

New Flowers

1 strand each 211, 340 and 3348 blended.

Draw smaller shapes and fill with colonial knots.

Leaves

2 strands 3346. Draw leaves and partial leaves amongst flowers and branches. Work in satin leaf stitch.

$\mathcal{L}$AVENDER (ITALIAN)

THREADS
208 lavender — very dark
522 fern green

550 violet — very dark
3740 antique violet — dark

Lavender Bush

branches and foliage — 2 strands 522. Lightly mark branches for the foliage. Start at top of bush and work each branch with fly stitch down to the 'ground'. Overlap some branches and stitch some smaller branches for a well-shaped bush. Fly stitch branches can only be worked down so you will have to finish off your thread at the 'ground' and start again. You can weave a short distance up the back for smaller branches.

stems — 1 strand each 522 and 3740 blended. Work straight stitch stems for the flowers at the top of the bush and amongst the foliage.

Flowers

flower heads — 1 strand each 550 and 3740 blended, bullion stitch (5 wraps). Attach to stems.

bracts — 2 strands 208, straight stitch. Add petal-like bracts to flower heads.

$\mathcal{P}$ETUNIA

THREADS
333 blue violet — very dark
340 blue violet — medium

3078 golden yellow — very light
3346 hunter green
3363 pine green — medium

Flowers

The shade of petunias can vary on one plant. Work some flowers in each colour with 1 strand of thread.

flowers — 1 strand 333, 1 strand 340. Draw circular shapes with a dot in the centre for the flowers. Petunias have 5 indentations around the flower. Buttonhole stitch around the flower leaving small space in the centre. Work 3 or 4 short stitches then 1 long stitch, 5 times. Join by stitching into first stitch.

centre — 2 strands 3078. Add a firm french knot to the centre of the flowers, tucking it in well.

Leaves

1 strand each 3346 and 3363 blended, lazy daisy stitch.

$\mathscr{P}$INKS

THREADS
503 blue green — medium
522 fern green

3608 plum — very light
3803 rose mauve

Flowers

2 strands 3608. Draw small circles with dot in centre for flowers. Work flowers with straight stitch from outside edge down into centre. All stitches are worked into same hole in centre. Do not work too many stitches for each flower and vary length of stitches to achieve a ragged edge like a carnation.

flecks — 2 strands 3803. Add flecks of deep pink around centre of flower with tiny back-stitches.

Stems

1 strand each 503 and 522 blended. Work short stems for flowers with stem stitch.

Leaves and stalks for buds

1 strand each 503 and 522. Add straight stitch leaves up and down stems and from the 'ground', between the stems. Some of these straight stitches will form stalks for buds.

Buds

1 strand each 503 and 522 blended. Add some buds to the stalks with tiny lazy daisy stitch.

$\mathscr{R}$OSE 'PETER FRANKENFELD'

THREADS

602 cranberry — medium
603 cranberry

604 cranberry — light
611 drab brown — dark
3051 green grey — dark

Branches
2 strands 611, stem stitch.

Flowers
Vary roses by directing the 3 centre bullions at an
angle and adding more bullions around 1 side of
rose than the other.

centre — 2 strands 602. Start in centre with deep-
est pink and work 3 bullion stitches (7 wraps) side by side.
second row — 2 strands 603. Work 5 bullion stitches with 603 (9 wraps)
around centre to overlap each other.
outer rows — 2 strands 604. Work 5 to 7 bullions (11 wraps).
stems (if needed) — 2 strands 3051, couching.

Buds
2 strands 602. Place 2 bullion stitches (7 wraps) side by side.
calyx and stem — 2 strands 3051. Work fly stitch around each bud.
Extend tail to form stem, couch in place. Add 2 sepals with straight
stitches to buds.

Leaves
2 strands 3051. Work curving stalks with backstitch. Add lazy daisy stitch
leaves in pairs plus 1 for the tip.

Other colour combinations: dusty pink — 3328, 760, 761; yellow —
725, 726, 3078.

ℛOSE GRASS OR ROSY POSY

THREADS
316 antique mauve — medium
718 plum

3363 pine green — medium
3607 plum — light

Flowers
1 strand 718, 1 strand of 3607. Some flowers are worked with 3607 and some with 718. Stitch them from centre with 6 very small lazy daisy stitches.

Stems
1 strand 316, couching.

Leaves
2 strands 3363. Work grass-like leaves between flowers with straight stitch.

$\mathcal{S}$AILOR-BOY DAISY

THREADS	*791 cornflower blue — very dark*
blanc neige	*3346 hunter green*
452 shell grey — medium	*3363 pine green — medium*

Flowers

petals — 2 strands blanc neige. Lightly mark flowers with outer circle and dot for centre. Do not make them too small. Divide the outer circle into quarters like a clock face. Work 1 straight stitch from the outside down into centre (leave small space for centre) for each quarter-hour and then fill in between these with 3 or 4 more straight stitch petals of uneven length, making 18-20 petals. Some petals will be stitched into same hole.

centre — 3 strands 791, french knot.

petal underside — 2 strands 452. Daisy undersides are tinged blue. To depict a closing flower or side-view flower, work a few straight stitch petals with 452.

odd petals — 1 strand 452, straight stitch. Add 3 or 4 odd petals to each daisy.

Stems

1 strand each 3363 and 3346 blended, straight stitch.

Leaves

1 strand each 3363 and 3346 blended, lazy daisy stitch.

Other colour combinations: The pink form of this daisy can be worked with 3609 for petals and 3042 for underside.

$\mathcal{V}$IOLET

THREADS
327 violet — very dark
743 yellow — medium
3346 hunter green

Leaves

1 strand 3346. Draw several heart-shaped leaves and work in buttonhole stitch. Start at top left-hand side of leaf and work in anti-clockwise direction with all stitches being worked into same hole.

Flowers

petals — 1 strand 327. Add violet flowers with 3 tiny lazy daisy stitch petals pointing downwards, and 2 lazy daisy stitch petals pointing upwards. Leave just a thread of fabric in centre of flower.
centres — 2 strands 743, french knots.

Bud

1 strand 327. Work buds with 2 lazy daisy stitches pointing downwards to the side.

Stems

1 strand 3346, stem stitch or backstitch. It is not necessary to give every flower a stem.
calyx — 1 strand 3346, fly stitch.

Other flower colours: 333 or 552.

WISTERIA

THREADS
208 lavender — very dark
210 lavender — medium

640 beige grey — very dark
3013 khaki green — light
3348 yellow green — medium

Vine

vine — 2 strands 640. Mark and work in stem stitch.

Flowers

flower stalks — 2 strands 3348. Draw flower stalks falling from vine with outline for raceme. These should be long and pendulous. Work stalks with backstitch.

flowers — 3 strands 210, 1 strand each 208 and 210 blended, 2 strands 208. Fill in flower shapes with french knots in 3 thread combinations. Work over stems leaving a little bit of stalk free of french knots at top. Start at top of flower with 210. Work most of raceme with this lighter thread. Two thirds of the way down start adding in some of blended threads to merge, and then purple thread for tip.

Leaves

leaf stalks — 2 strands 3348. Mark curving leaf stalks from stems and work them with backstitch.

leaves — 1 strand each 3013 and 3348 blended. Add lazy daisy leaves to stalks. Leaves occur in pairs with 1 at the tip (9 to 11 leaves).

The Stitches

STEM STITCH

Working from left to right, take small, even, straight or slanting stitches along design line. Leave space between previous stitch and point where needle emerges. Keep thread below or on same side of work.

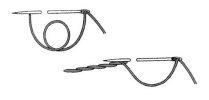

BACKSTITCH

Backstitch is useful to form a delicate line and for curves and outlines.

COUCHING

Short lengths of couching can be worked with one needle and one thread, but longer lengths require two needles and threads. They should both be kept on top of work to prevent tangling.

Lay thread along design line, holding and guiding its direction with your thumb. Tie down with small straight stitches made across it at regular intervals.

FRENCH KNOTS

Bring thread up at desired spot. Hold thread with your left hand. With needle pointing toward you, place under thread from left-hand side and twist it around once. Insert needle close to where thread first emerged, but not in same hole. Draw thread around needle to firm knot and pull through to back.

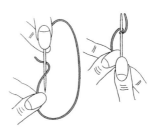

COLONIAL KNOTS

Bring thread up at desired spot. Hold thread with your left hand. With needle pointing away from you, place it under thread from the left-hand side and twist it in an anticlockwise direction back towards yourself. The needle will now be pointing at you. The second part of the stitch is same as for french knot.

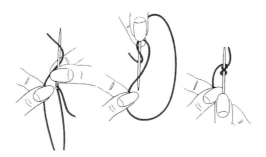

BULLION STITCH

This stitch should be worked with a straw or millinery needle. Commence as though to make a backstitch the required length for the bullion stitch. Bring needle up beside starting point but do not pull

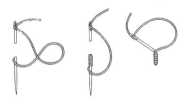

through. Wrap thread around needle, in a clockwise direction, the required number of times. Do not wrap too tightly. Place your left thumb over wraps, then pull needle through wraps. Insert needle beside starting point and pull through to complete bullion stitch.

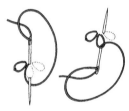

LAZY DAISY STITCH

Bring needle through at point where you wish to begin your stitch. Hold thread below your work and insert needle just beside where thread first emerged. Bring needle out at desired distance, keeping thread underneath. Fasten loop at end with a small stitch.

FLY STITCH

This is an open lazy daisy stitch. Bring needle through at top left of your design line. Insert needle a little distance away to the right and take a

small diagonal stitch to centre with thread below needle. Pull through and fasten with a straight downward stitch.

BUTTONHOLE STITCH

This can be worked in a row or a circle. Start on outside edge and work from left to right. Hold thread below and take a downward straight stitch and draw up with thread underneath needle. Continue in this way, spacing stitches as required.

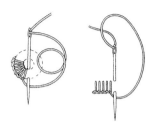

STRAIGHT STITCH

Straight stitch is a single satin stitch and can be worked in any direction and to any length.

SATIN LEAF STITCH

The first stitch should be a little longer than you might expect, to form a good point on leaf. Work first satin stitch from the point of the leaf back into the centre. Bring needle back up on the right of first stitch at the leaf tip. Take this second stitch back to central leaf vein and insert needle just below, but very close to first stitch. Work satin stitches alternately from each side fanning them as leaf forms. At same time, continue to work closely down central vein. You may need to add 1 or 2 extra stitches onto one side of the leaf.

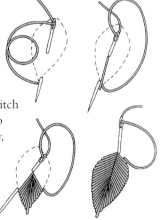

Finishing

When you think you have finished stitching your embroidered piece, look at it carefully to make sure it is balanced. Pin it up on a curtain and look at it from a distance. You will probably find you need to add an extra flower or leaf here and there.

Be sure to sign and date your finished embroidery. To do this, use 1 strand of thread in a light shade and work with small stitches in stem or backstitch.

Tidy up the threads at the back, trimming back so there are no long tags that will show at the front.

WASHING

I find my embroidery is quite grubby by the time it is finished and really needs washing. Carefully hand-wash in warm water with soft soap. Don't soak it as some deep-shaded threads may bleed. Any stubborn pencil marks can be removed with a toothbrush. Rinse the embroidery well, but don't wring, as creases are difficult to remove.

PRESSING

It is best to iron your embroidery as soon as it is washed. Place a towel on the ironing board and overlay with a pressing cloth. Place the wet embroidery face down on the towels. You can either place another cloth over the embroidery, or iron it direct, but please take care not to scorch it.

Now for the exciting bit! When you turn the embroidery over you will see your embroidered flowers come to life.